Tweetings

@doctor_rhonda

Words of Wisdom for Life's Journey

Rhonda Wells-Wilbon

Pearly Gates Publishing LLC
INSPIRING CHRISTIAN AUTHORS TO BE AUTHORS

Pearly Gates Publishing, LLC, Harlem, GA (USA)

Tweetings @doctor_rhonda

Published by Pearly Gates Publishing, LLC
P.O. Box 639, Harlem, GA 30814 USA
832.994.8797 | www.pearlygatespublishing.com

Cover design by Rodrigo Adolfo
Interior design by Honeylette Pino

Published in the United States of America
1st Ed. ISBN 13: 978-1-62902-066-2
2nd Ed. ISBN 13: 978-0-9815233-1-6

1. Self-Help / Personal Growth / General
2. Self-Help / Motivational & Inspirational
13.09.16 1st Edition
22.11.17 2nd Edition

Dedication

For **Azaan** and **Jabari**

You are my
JaJa
"Gift from God"

Introduction

Words, speech, and language are, in many ways, the most powerful tools we have to negotiate life. Those who learn how to use, define, and redefine words give voice to all that is within that the eyes cannot see.

These affirmations have been compiled from my tweets. Tweeting gives me a platform on which to share some of the words of wisdom that flow through me. It is my hope that they will find even greater meaning when shared with others.

I hope *Tweetings* will help affirm your voice.

dr rhonda

Your name defines
your life's work
and your contribution
to The Universe.

I am Rhonda –
"a powerful river"
Paving the way,
Moving through
Space and time,
Unfolding the source
Of my power.
Who are you?

True vision sees from within.

Every day begins
and ends
with
the Sun.

I'm like
a ship sailing,
looking for
a place
to call home.

I serve a risen Savior.
The righteousness of
His grace & mercy
cover me
every single day
of my amazing life.

I'm dancing in the rain.
Nothing will ever stop me.

Be very cautious
of what is gained
at the expense of others.

Love doesn't need permission to come,
but it does need you to work
in order to stay.

Walk into the light.

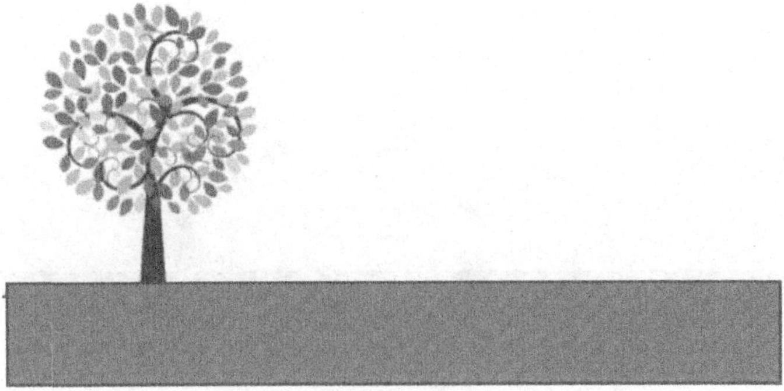

No one else has to be weak
in order for you to be strong.

Life is intended
To be filled with
The opportunity
To be in the
Spirit of God.

Today I am releasing bad habits,
negative energy, and harmful people
that keep me from breaking through
to my greatest possibility.

Liberty & justice
is my birthright.

Dreams are always coming true.
What you believe in your mind's eye
is what will be the reality
of your life tomorrow,
so dream.

Stand tall…you won't fall.
God's got it!

Think positive.
Think peace.
Think purpose.
Thoughts are
the source
of all that is possible.

What I exhale
is what I give to
The Universe.

It takes less time and energy
to build yourself up
than it does
to break others down.
You be the light,
especially in dark places.

If the express lane isn't moving,
is it still the express lane?
If your life isn't moving,
get in another lane.

When we lose our focus,
God always has a way of
blocking the paths we
shouldn't be on…
and clearing the paths
we should be on.

Always respect the will of
The Universe.

Ever seen a situation taking a nosedive,
start praying, and then watch God turn
the whole thing around right before you?

You be the reason someone
grew, changed, healed, forgave…
and found God
at the cutting edge of
what seemed to be a
rainbow's end.

Even The Universe bows
to the Great I Am.

I'm still learning how to unwant
people who don't want me.

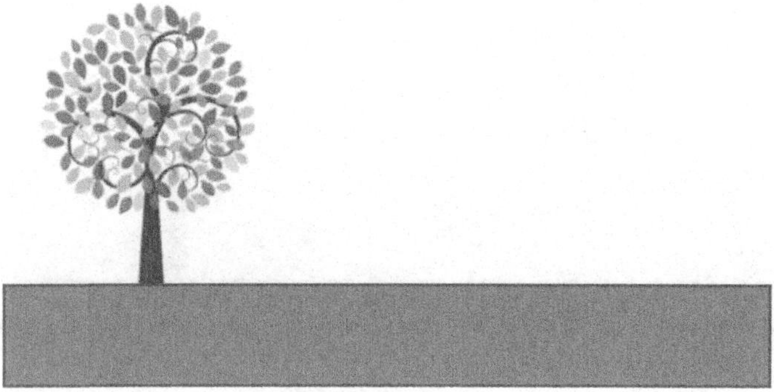

I'm just coming to the full understanding
of how much courage it takes to walk away
from someone who doesn't really love you.

When you open your heart, the magnificent beauty of life shines from within, and a breakthrough to bright beginnings unfolds.

No one can give you more than
they have…including you.
Expectations can't be greater
than what is possible.

Don't limit your positive energy
just for the special people in your life.
Share it abundantly and
anticipate generous returns.

Sometimes, all you can do is
dance in the rain.

When I connect in harmony
with the gift of love,
nothing in life is more.

All I ever wanted was
someone to call my own…
someone who loved me back…
someone not afraid to give.

Protect me with your wisdom…
cover me with your love.

I am my dream maker.

When it comes to true love,
there is no competition and
no one keeps score.
Love always gives
the best it possibly can.

I am weaker than I realized,
yet the Keeper
kept me through it all.

Save the very worst of who you are
and the very best of who you are
just for you.

There's something about being true,
authentic, faithful, real, and brutally honest
that just turns everyone off.

When people want us to be less than
our authentic selves,
ask yourself,
"Who are these people and
how can I move beyond where they are?"

If there are shackles on my thinking
causing me to live in fear,
I am the only one who can set me free.

Love is there when everything else fails.
Be love, be light, be happy…
Dare to live life
in the space of all your possibility.

Grow, change, and stay strong.
The ending of what has been
is your new beginning.

It is not wise to rescue people
from the lessons they must learn.

Love is unexplainable…
but it never leaves you void.

If someone you love finds
happiness without you,
let them.

When you keep the faith,
focus on the positive, and
believe in what is possible,
life always returns to
the power of the circle.

Enabling people is not helping them;
it is disempowering and oppressive.
We all have to be empowered
to receive life's lessons.

There is something
so beautiful and amazing
about dancing
to the beat
of your own heart,
in harmony
with someone
who loves you back.

The spirit of who I am
is much greater
than anything
your eyes can see.

When I speak the truth,
it is so that I can live in peace.
An unauthentic life
is not a life worth living.

Love never gives up,
but it also never
holds you hostage.

Today, be true
to what you know is true
and who you know will be true
to you.
An authentic life
is the best life to live.

We all have the capacity to exist
on the dark side of sanity.
For so many,
being mentally healthy
requires work.
Do the work.

When I stretch,
I realize
my wings are bigger
than I ever thought they'd be,
and they can take me to places
I never thought I'd go.

Even the clouds bend
to the sun.

Even when I'm not sure
I'm doing
what I'm supposed to do,
I still am who
I'm supposed to be.
Never be confused
about who you are.

I keep honoring my commitment
to a mystery called love.

Fathers, cover your children.
It is the most important protection
they will ever have,
and it is never too late.

When it's all over,
All you leave behind
Are your relationships.
What will be your legacy?

In the end,
all our fears turn into
pieces of the puzzle –
all necessary to
understand the fullness of life.

I'm determined to be sane.
How about you?

I'm gonna keep giving
because my gifts come from
a Divine Creator
who expects me to honor my purpose.

The joy I have is magnified
when I share it with others.

Be careful around people
who get power from
breaking you down.

Life is short,
yet each day is filled
with so much possibility.
Today, I hope
you reach the impossible.

When you see others'
blessings coming,
rise with the waves.

Persistence breaks down walls.

A new door to something fabulous
is around the corner…
just keep moving.

It is not possible to find
happiness in sad places.
Be a magnet
for the energy you desire.

Today, spread all that is
good, positive, beautiful, and amazing
about you…
everywhere you go.

Living a righteous life is not easy,
but it is the right thing to do.
As you move in that spirit,
The Universe honors your obedience.

If you want to move
opposition out of your way,
speak authority over your life.

In the image of the rising sun,
you were created to shine.

You have a right to heal
from old wounds,
laugh until you cry,
dance in the rain,
and love again.

If you let go of old things,
you will bloom
and be magnificently blessed.

When you are blessed with an
opportunity to love somebody
and be loved back in return,
assume it is meant to be.

Be the best of who you say you are.

Plant your love
in relationships
that have the capacity to grow.

If you fall apart every time
someone doesn't get you,
where would you be?

Don't let unhealthy people
drag you into the darkness.

Miracles are at the cutting edge
of what you're doing
and what you're afraid to do.

If it is in line with your purpose, it will be…
If it is not, no matter how hard you try,
it will NEVER work out right.

Today, surrender to all the things
that make you smile.

Always embrace your true voice.
Every morning has tremendous promise.

When someone you care about is fragile,
don't wait until they're broken
to help them get help.

You are chosen to be in service
To the destiny of others.

I am a product of my past,
a reality of my present,
and the hope of all my
possibilities tomorrow.

When someone isn't with you in the
right spiritual space,
it is difficult for them to give you
what you need and want.

When someone keeps asking you for something
you never give them, and they finally stop,
it's not over.
They will never forget.

Mental health is a national health crisis.
We all have an investment in supporting
the mental health of others…
and ourselves.

What you put into life
always comes back to you.

If you believe in freedom,
then have the courage
to stop oppressing others
and the strength
to stand up for yourself.

If someone loves you, let them.

In spite of us,
The Universe is always
working in our favor…
And so, it is.

If there is even a flicker of light in you,
let it shine
for someone in darkness to see.

Have you ever needed someone to help
you regain your balance?
I understand…
The Universe understands.

Starting over was always a part
of the original plan.

To Him who rescues and restores me
every day…
I give thanks.

Every day, be reborn again…
Reflect, rebuild, regain, renew, restore,
and rejoice.
Celebrate the possibility of a new you.

We look to others to light a path that
leads the way, and The Universe
depends on us to be the light
that is the way.

Remember: You belong to the positive
poetry of The Universe.

Actually, sometimes it is all about you.

You will surpass when you let go.

Hurt people not ready to heal
are drawn to hurt people
who will help them hurt.
Hurt people ready to heal
are drawn to healers
who help them heal.

Survival is not the final stage of being;
it is only a stage in the process.

Choose to be intentional
about your choices.

If you don't work at it,
nothing will work.

I'm not just a survivor,
I'm a miracle.

My faith is the foundation
from where I thrive.

I am the reason my ancestors survived,
and I am proud to be a bridge
for the next generation of survivors.

Speak truth into The Universe…
someone is listening.

When I say this isn't a good time,
trust me.

When the energy isn't right for you,
have the wisdom to walk away.

The healers before me
left big shoes to fill,
but also broad shoulders
on which I stand.

If I keep my focus on what is possible,
I can't lose.

Never stop moving in the direction
of your greatness.

It is true that
each day is an opportunity
to start over,
but never forget
every day counts.

Light always wins over darkness.

No matter your condition
or situation in life,
every day is an opportunity
to give thanks.

If you own who you are,
No one can disempower you.

Journeying home
is the source of all you need
to reflect,
forgive,
restore,
heal, and
regain new strength
to journey on.

There are some things in life
that can't be fully explained.
You have to live it to find
true meaning and understanding.

We all have choices.
Deciding to do nothing is a choice.

If I fall…
I'm going to get up.

Today, I rededicated myself
to my own wellness
so that I can be an example
in my service to others.

It's not love if it doesn't set you free.

The old stuff is over.
Letting go
is the only way
for the new stuff
to find you.

Every day has only 24 hours.
When you've done
all the things
you had to do,
how much time
did you leave
to just be?

Your own need for self-empowerment
is not accomplished
by disempowering and controlling others.
Life's balance is not a struggle.

Don't wait for vacation…
Do something fun…
Even if just for a moment…
Every day.

The wall I never wanted
to build around myself
Keeps getting higher…
and higher…
and higher.

Even when I say no,
I reserve the right
to change my mind
at any time
and say yes.

Even when I say yes,
I reserve the right
to change my mind
at any time
and say no.

Giving and receiving works
when no one gives more
than they receive and
receives no more
than they give.

Stop being
who you think
you should be
and just be
who you are.

Blessed beyond measure.

Today, live in the moment,
do something fun,
spend time with someone exciting,
have dessert first,
and fall asleep with a smile.

No matter the current space
you are in,
when God puts powerful
people and energy
around you,
walk in the victory
that is already yours.

Today, I surrender to my greatness.

In the face of adversity and challenge,
The Universe doesn't stop doing what it
was created to do.
Why should you?

Just blessed…
What else can I say?

Tell me again:
Why are you not living your dreams?

More healing,
more blessings,
more change…
They're on the way.

I can't change anything
but the way I think
and what I do.

Something is always blooming.

Today, I've noticed
that all the crazy stuff
from yesterday…
it has just moved
out of my way.

I've discovered
that every day
is a new opportunity
to be fabulous.

God, I don't wanna learn
any more lessons…
but I'm sure
You have more to teach me
anyway.

The battle isn't over,
but today, I'm dancing
in the sunlight and
stomping all over my enemies.

Moving beyond possibility…
Walking in victory…
Nothing can stop me.

My ancestors
survived the tragedy
of enslavement
so that I could value
family, culture,
working together,
and forgiveness.

You are always closer
than you think you are.
But even more,
you are always stronger
than you have ever been.

So glad every day is an opportunity to
start anew and reclaim one's destiny.

No matter how much they hurt,
wounds will heal…
and so will you.

Every time I say yes,
God delivers me into a new victory.

Seasons are constantly changing,
making a major shift
four times every year.
How often do you change?

Respect and embrace
the change in every season.

Be careful who you follow.
They may not know
how to get to
where you are going.

I have to be who I say I am.

I'm learning that
nothing I do
makes any sense
if it is not a part
of my divine purpose.

Sometimes, the walls we build
to protect ourselves
actually keep our blessings
from getting in.

Perfecting my own self-healing
and teaching others how to discover
the path to their self-healing
is my gift from The Universe.

I'm waiting for old doors
to finally close
so the new doors
to a divine destiny
can finally open.

Some days, the old scars and wounds
hurt as much as they did
when they were brand-new.

God's grace and mercy cover me
every single day of my amazing life.
Those who move against me
have no idea what they're up against.

Rise with your commitment to
"be on purpose,"
and God will do the rest.

Don't ever lose your voice.

Always remember to give and receive
love from those who see
the very best in you.

Today's crazy stuff
has nothing to do with you.
God just needs your light
in some dark places.

Protect yourself.
Get rid of toxic relationships
immediately.

Stand still and
God will
make the space
you are in…
your space.

There is no disconnection between physical, mental, and spiritual health unless we allow the pieces of ourselves to function in disharmony.

I am moving in the spirit
of my divine greatness.

Do not be afraid
of what appears to be a lion.
He is not real,
but a creation of
his own imagination.

Move into the spirit of your possibility
every single morning you rise.

I don't believe in impossibility based on
current reality because The Universe
is constantly shifting in my favor.

We keep waiting for God to open a door,
and He keeps waiting for us
to just walk through.

Healing is a deliberate and
necessary choice each of us must
make for the victory of us all.

Rise every day and decide to be sane.

What we do together
inside the circle
will last forever!!!

We have the right to speak
our own truths into existence.

Live in the spirit of forgiveness
so that you might realize
the healing power of the circle.

Our relationships with each other
are critically important.
We must have the capacity to forgive
and seek forgiveness from others.

May the peace and joy of God's
love and mercy for you
shine for the entire world to see.

I am aware that often,
the lessons I teach others
are the lessons I need to know
and accept for myself.

Who are you?
And how do you know you are
who you say you are?

God, please help me.
I have been at this major crossroad
much too long.

Are the things I desire in life
really the things I need?

If I could give you the best parts of me,
I'd give you my smile, my hugs, my kisses,
my heart, my soul, and my intellect.
Most of all, I'd give you my love.

Jesus teaches us how to live through
challenging times, be crucified,
suffer death, and get up and rise again.

Yesterday, today, and tomorrow
are the only three days on my calendar.
I can't dwell on the past,
yet I don't want to get ahead of the miracles
God is waiting to reveal to me today.

Discipline must be related to
the outcome you desire.

Seeds won't thrive without soil.

My mission has to be my life's focus.

We can't really know what other people believe;
we can only speak to their actions.
Our interpretation of their actions
may not be a true reflection of their intent.

Intend to "be" on purpose.

The greatest gift
you can give yourself
is self-discipline.

It is good to be bold,
Brilliant, and beautiful.

When God opens the floodgates of understanding
and blessings, you will not remember all the
negative things you went through to get to
your great day of enlightenment.

Just walk into your morning
—your great day—
with excellence, peace, glory, thanksgiving,
freedom, happiness, understanding,
salvation, truth, justice, balance, harmony,
purpose, compassion, and righteousness.

I am moving in the spirit
of my divine purpose.

I surrender to the unfolding of
a space and time, created to embrace
the beautiful gift that is me.

I must replenish, rebuild, renew, reclaim,
restore, and rejoice.
Gonna try again to laugh, smile, trust, forgive,
surrender, love, and connect to what is possible.

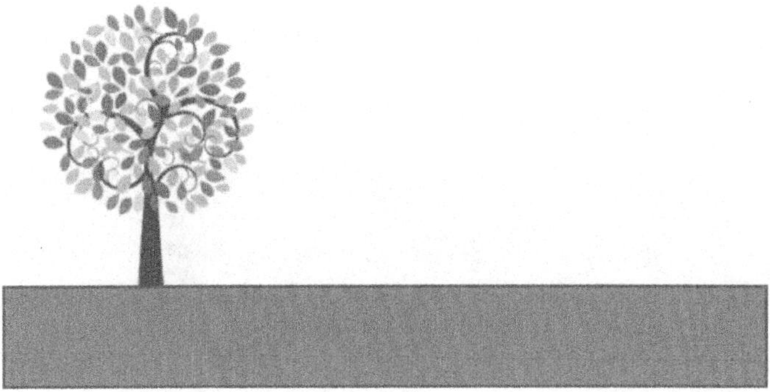

Endings pave the way
for new beginnings.

Darkness can only exist
in the shadows of the light.

I am a walking, breathing miracle,
passing through space and time,
caught between the unknown and reality,
looking for a place to call my own.

What we do "On Purpose"
is always in divine order.
Its righteousness shines brightly,
even when we feel no one sees.
It is our lifeline to The Universe,
our ancestors, our seed, and our God.

Living on purpose is how we fulfill our destiny.
Moving in our destiny brings forth such a
brilliant light, often, others cannot see.

There's still time to live an amazing life
on your own terms
to receive unconditional love…
to inhale and exhale life deeply.

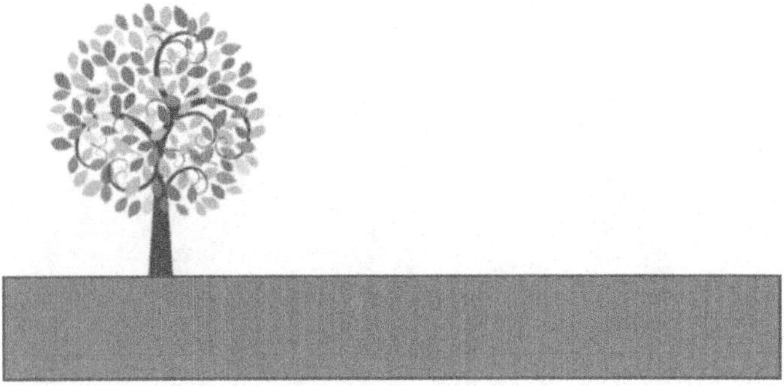

Make time to take in deeply
the moments that take
your breath away
because we never ever
get a chance to live
those moments again.

I AM
laying a Your feet,
covered by Your wisdom,
protected by Your truth,
and enjoying every moment of my journey.

Relief can only come
when healing begins.

Heal from your harms
so that you are not a harm
to yourself and others.

Today, I decided to stop doing all the things
that made me sad or weren't helping me grow.
Today, I found balance from deep within.

You honor my strength by allowing me
to have moments of weakness.

What I exhale
is what I give
to The Universe.

Great trees live forever.

No one and nothing has the power
to separate me from my greatness,
my purpose, or my destiny.

Change—like emotional and spiritual healing—
is a deliberate and necessary choice.
We must liberate ourselves,
be instruments of change for others,
and hold ourselves and each other accountable.

I'm so glad I know whose I am 24/7.

There is nothing greater
than my divine purpose.

I cannot fail.

When I am oppressed,
it is so I can rise and live again.

I'm not mad about anything the enemy
does against me or the negative energy
that surrounds my current life situation.
I'm just waiting for God's revelation.

Made in the USA
Monee, IL
04 November 2026

67386981R00134